This is a partial compilation of things I received from Abba as I met with Him mostly in the wee hours of the morning. These are written in the simplest and most elementary form, and speak of God's call on our lives, His relentless pursuit of our lives, and the battles we fight to hold on to the lives He has given us.

Amara Alexander

My Rhema Inspirations Presents

DOWNLOADS FROM HEAVEN

"When you think they're just your thoughts, think again. They could very well be *downloads from heaven*"

XULON PRESS

Xulon Press
2301 Lucien Way #415
Maitland, FL 32751
407.339.4217
www.xulonpress.com

© 2020 by Amara Alexander

All rights reserved solely by the author. The author guarantees all contents are original and do not infringe upon the legal rights of any other person or work. No part of this book may be reproduced in any form without the permission of the author. The views expressed in this book are not necessarily those of the publisher.

Unless otherwise indicated, Scripture quotations taken from the Holy Bible, New Living Translation (NLT). Copyright ©1996, 2004, 2007 by Tyndale House Foundation. Used by permission of Tyndale House Publishers, Inc.

Scripture quotations taken from the King James Version (KJV) – *public domain.*

Scripture quotations taken from the New King James Version (NKJV). Copyright © 1982 by Thomas Nelson, Inc. Used by permission. All rights reserved.

Scripture quotations taken from The Message (MSG). Copyright © 1993, 1994, 1995, 1996, 2000, 2001, 2002. Used by permission of NavPress Publishing Group. Used by permission. All rights reserved.

Scripture quotations taken from the Holy Bible, New International Version (NIV). Copyright © 1973, 1978, 1984, 2011 by Biblica, Inc.™. Used by permission. All rights reserved.

Scripture quotations taken from the English Standard Version (ESV). Copyright © 2001 by Crossway, a publishing ministry of Good News Publishers. Used by permission. All rights reserved.

Section Three image by ricardo-cruz-pKMFZmVHsNk-unsplash300
All other images are sole property of the author

Printed in the United States of America.

Paperback ISBN-13: 978-1-6628-0229-4
eBook ISBN-13: 978-1-6628-0230-0

Dedication

I dedicate this book to my Heavenly Father who encouraged me often saying, *"this time keep going"*. Even at times when I felt that I was paddling up stream, against the current, with only one paddle and my boat slowly but steadily filling with water, He said, **"this time keep going"**. So I did.

Thank You Daddy!

Table of Contents

Section 1: The Rescue
1. Breathe With Me 2
2. These Scars 5
3. What You Didn't Get............................7
4. You Know Me, Still..............................9
5. Deal Breaker.................................... 10
6. Finally Happy Me 12
7. Moving On 14
8. I Still Have Room 15
9. I Will Wait 17
10. What's In a Name? 19
11. Deep Wounds 24

Section 2: The Call
1. I'm So Pregnant................................ 30
2. Ten Virgins 33
3. God Cares....................................... 36
4. God Is in the People Business 38
5. Silent Witness 40
6. God Is Not Out to Get You 41
7. The F-ing Truth 43
8. Growing 45
9. Not Stunted, Just Delayed 46
10. She Came 48
11. The Church Has Left the Building 50
12. I Just Have To Be Available................... 52
13. The Grand Canyon Lightbulb Moment 54
14. Stood Up..57

Section 3: The Battles We Fight

1. 2020 Vision 64
2. Run Toward Your Fear......................... 65
3. Rhu...67
4. Every Truth Don't Have to Be Told 68
5. The Victory Is In Your Mouth 70
6. Between Your Head and Your Heart Lies Your Mouth 72
7. The Art of Waiting 73
8. A Roar Too Loud to Ignore 76
9. Brokenness Continuum......................... 79
10. Distract, Discourage, Destroy 80
11. Don't Let This Melanin Fool You................ 83
12. False Evidence Appearing Real 88
13. The Verbal Arsonist........................... 90

Section 4: God Is

1. The Help 96
2. God, You Are...................................97
3. Relentless Love 99
4. God Speaks Ebonics........................... 101
5. God Understands Rap......................... 102
6. No Pumping Necessary 103
7. Er-Body Talkin' Bout Goliath 105
8. Act-Ing Out Prayer 112

Introduction and Bio

My purpose for this book of poetry and short writing pieces, is first and foremost to represent Jesus, Holy Spirit, and the Father in the most favorable light as I know how. Secondly it is to show the different phases of our relationship with our Father. Starting with the rescue He has already set in place to save us from certain death, to the call He has placed on our lives to join Him in His work, to the battles we fight with Him leading us to victory, straight through to just knowing and loving Him for Who He is and always will be. The Author and Finisher of our faith.

Section One

With every bone in my body I will praise Him:
Lord who can compare with You?
Who else rescues the helpless from the strong?
Who else protects the helpless and poor from those
who rob them?
(Psalm 35:10 [New Living Translation])

The Rescue

God Is Not Out To Get You...Or Is He?

Breathe With Me

I know it's hard right now but inhale...now exhale
The air is stiff and stale and does not want to move
But even though the air is stagnant, take it in...now let it out
I will be your breathing coach so to speak

Feel the air began to circulate in your lungs again
Whatever took your breath away does not control you
You feel that your wind has been cut off and you'll never breathe again
But I speak life to you, now breathe with Me

You say you've never felt pain like this before
It pierced your heart and took your breath away
You take a deep breath in and hold on
Because letting go means you'll feel again

It hurts to breathe. Oxygen means life
And right now, you just want to die
You feel that living is such a waste of time
Just using up air. Just occupying space

Like quicksand it tried to pull you under
It tried to suffocate you and take your life away
But just before you succumbed under its power
I snatched you up and out, and breathed air into your lungs

So, breathe with Me, I know it's hard right now
One breath at a time, inhale....now, exhale
Feel the stale air moving out and the fresh moving in
Feel the air began to move in and out of your lungs again

There's no injustice you've suffered that I didn't suffer first
I went before you so I could be your breathing coach
There is life after hurt and it begins with Me
Now let go and let Me teach you to breathe again

I have conquered that thing that took your breath away
I have come that you might have renewed life
Replacing pain with purpose day by day
If you breathe with Me, I'll breathe on you.

> *"For the Spirit of God has made me, And the **breath** of the Almighty gives me life" (Job 33:4 [New Living Translation])*

Ezekial 37: 4-14 says; Again, He said to me, "Prophesy over these bones and say to them, "O dry bones, hear the word of the Lord'. Thus, says the Lord to these bones, Behold I will cause **breath** to enter you that you may come to life. I will put sinews on you, make flesh grow back on you, cover you with skin and put **breath** in you that you may come alive, and you will know that I Am the Lord". So I prophesied as I was commanded, and as I prophesied, there was a noise, and behold, a rattling, and the bones came together, bone to its bone. And I looked and behold, sinews were on them, and flesh grew and skin covered them, but there was no **breath** in them. Then He said to me, Prophesy to the **breath**, prophesy son of man, and say to the **breath**, "Thus says the Lord GOD, Come from the four winds, O **breath**, and **breathe** on these slain, that they come to life.

So I prophesied as He commanded me, and **breath** came into them, and they came to life and stood on their feet, an exceedingly great army. Then He said to me, "Son of man, these bones are the whole house of Israel, behold they say, 'Our bones have dried up and our hope has perished, we are completely cut off'.

"Therefore prophesy and say to them, Thus says the Lord GOD, Behold I will open your graves and cause you to come up out of your graves My people and I will bring you into the land of Israel. "Then you will know that I Am the Lord when I have opened your graves and caused you to come up out of your graves. My people, I will put My Spirit within you, and you will come to life, and I will place you in your own land. Then you will know that I the Lord have spoken and done it, declares the Lord.

These Scars

Behind every scar there is a story
They tell of the storms you've been through
They testify of the battles you've fought
While Jesus fought beside you

You're never alone in this battle
Though wounds you will attain
Jesus would never leave you alone
No matter how great the pain

Between every scar there is clear skin
That hasn't been injured or scarred
Those are the times when war is at rest
The times when the battle's not hard

Without the scars your wounds would be open
Uncovered to the world and exposed
Though scars are not pretty, they serve a great purpose
They cover, protect and they close

A few battle scars you got this round
You fought with faith and won
You trusted Him to supply your strength
This soldier will not run

So don't be grieved about your scars
Don't drop your head in shame
Thank God for every scar you bare
Thank God in Jesus name

> *"For our light afflictions, which is for but a moment, worketh for us a far more exceeding and eternal weight of glory" (I Corinthians 4:17 [King James Version])*

> *"Fight the good fight of faith, lay hold on eternal life, whereunto thou art also called, and hast professed a good profession before many witnesses" (I Timothy 6:12 [KJV])*

What You Didn't Get

Have you felt that you weren't blessed because of what you didn't get?

Have you coveted your neighbor's life, looked at yours with regret?

Did you say that should have been me with that house, that job, that car?

Did you say that I've out prayed them by a mile this year so far?

Why does it seem that they're so blessed and I'm so far behind?

I prayed to God for that same thing by rights that should be mine

I feel like what I did not get has caused me great distress

I did not get the things I want so am I really blessed?

Then a voice from heaven said, My child please do not fret

I've got a list of things for you, things that you did not get

You didn't get that heart transplant that knew you by your name

It called you out one evening but I sent it off in shame.

That car accident that was waiting for you on twenty ninth and Pine?

I sent you back home to get your notes, yes that delay was Mine

You didn't get that lay off that was promised you last week

I gave you favor with your boss while others met defeat

Dialysis passed you by, then cancer came knocking at your door
I stopped it, blocked it, held it back, yes that was Me for sure
Confusion tried to cloud your mind depression tried to take you out
I lifted My standard against your foe, you came back strong without a doubt
So if your mind attempts to force you back into that place
Remind your heart to tell your mind that it was by My grace
That held back things that you deserved, things that you could not see
The things you didn't get were small when compared to My grace and mercy

> *"But in Your great mercy you did not put an end to them or abandon them, for You are a gracious and merciful God" (Nehemiah 9:31 [New International Version])*

> *"Rejoice always, pray continually, give thanks in all circumstances, for this is God's will for you in Christ Jesus" (I Thessalonians 5: 16-18 [NIV])*

If we looked at being blessed from a different perspective, maybe we would see the benefits of what we **did not** receive. If you didn't get the wife, the husband, the ministry, etc. that you desired, could it be the Father is protecting you?

You Know Me, Still

You know me still you love me
naked am I before You
trapped inhibitions set free
all illusions, all delusions removed
You know me yet still You love me

"But now thus saith the Lord that created thee, O Jacob, and He that formed thee O Israel, Fear not: for I have redeemed thee, I have called thee by thy name; thou art mine" (Isaiah 43:1 [King James Version])

Deal Breaker
All My Single Ladies

You like to worldly party, but I don't
You like the fast life, but I don't
You like to cheat a little, but I don't
You like to lie a little, but I don't
You like to brag and show off, but I don't
You put your trust in self, but I don't
You like to fornicate a little, but I don't...at all

I have a job, but you don't
I have a car, but you don't
I value relationships, but you don't
I watch what I say, but you don't
I respect you, but you don't
I enjoy life, but you don't
I have integrity, but you don't
I love God, but you don't
DEAL BREAKER!!!!!

> *"Do not team up with those who are unbelievers. How can righteousness be a partner with wickedness? How can light live with darkness?" (2 Corinthians 6:14 [New Living Translation])*

"Do not be deceived: Evil communication corrupts good manners" (I Corinthians 15:33 [King James Version])

"Do not be misled: Bad company corrupts good character" (I Corinthians 15:33 [New International Version])

Finally Happy Me

It took me some time, some lessons, some intentional decisions
But I'm finally happy with who You made me to be
I know now that I don't have to be like him or her or them
It's good to know that I can just be me

The silly me, the creative me
The love to match my clothes, me
The not so fond of my hair, me
Thank You for who You made me to be

The stumbling awkwardly saying it, me
The spit it out better at writing it, me
The different from others is ok with You, me
Thank You for who You made me to be

The often very complicated, me
The dedicated loyal friend to the end, me
The learned I don't have to be in control, me
Thank You for who You made me to be, me

The believe God's Word with all my heart, me
The cry at the first phrase of a worship song, me
The precious apple of His eye, me
Thank You for who You made me to be

The love my family beyond words, me
The every memory, bad or good counts, me
The compelled to help people in distress, me
Thank You for who You made me to be

The hate to deal with liars, me
The fan of truth and integrity, me
The take a hundred photos a minute, me
Thank You for who You made me to be

The please wash your hands first, me
The write it in my journal, me
Just one of those 'ole' people God's got a hold on, me
Thank You for who You made me to be

Thank You for setting me free just to be
The person that You placed inside of me
Thank You my God that now I can see
You love me for who You made me to be

I AM THE ME THAT YOU MADE ME TO BE

"For You formed my inward parts; You knitted me together in my mother's womb. I praise You, for I am fearfully and wonderfully made. Wonderful are Your works. My soul knows it very well. My frame was not hidden from You, when I was being made in secret, intricately woven in the depths of the earth" (Psalm 139:13-15 [English Standard Version])

Moving On

Moving on from stupid thoughts that benefit nothing.
From anger and bitterness that can
poison and bring disease.
From "pity parties", whose guest are
compromising and uncomfortable.
From people who wag their heads in
agreement to my self-pitying complaints
I must move on or else I die. Dying is not an option.

"Like newborn babies, crave pure spiritual milk, so that by it you may grow up in your salvation, now that you have tasted that the Lord is good" (I Peter 2:2-3 [New International Version])

"When I was a child, I talked like a child, I thought like a child, I reasoned like a child. When I became a man, I put away childish ways" (I Corinthians 13:11 [NIV]

I Still Have Room

All of my life that's behind me is inside me. And I still have room for more.
More lessons to learn, more assignments to conquer, more relationships to build.
Yes, I still have room for more

All of my life that's behind me is within me. And I still have room for more.
More joys to enjoy, more fears to overcome, more disappointments to overlook.
Yes, I still have room for more.

All of my life that's behind me is inside me. And I still have room for more.
More shouts of praise, more childlike amazement, to a God that never fails.
Yes, I still have room for more.

All of my life that's behind me is within me. And I still have room for more.
More understanding to attain, more forgiveness to give, more of both on a two-way street.
Yes, I still have room for more.

All of my life that's behind me is inside me. And I still have room for more.

More thoughts to think, more love to give, more life to live, more life to live, more life to live

Yes, I still have room.

> *"Teach us to realize the brevity of life, so that we may grow in wisdom" (Psalm 90:12 [New International Version])*

I Will Wait

When I want to run ahead of You because I think I know what's best
I feel You gently tugging at my spirit, "settle down, just rest"
So many anxious thoughts just whirling about inside my head
And sleep won't come no matter how still I lie when I'm in bed
I can hear You telling me "slow down, I'm in control"
"Just place your hand inside My hand and never break your hold"
The clock is ticking moving forward, time waits for no man
"I Am the Lord, I have all power, even time is in My hands"
Twiddling my thumbs and patting my feet, wishing You'd hurry along
You say, "if I do what you ask right now, everything would go all wrong"
"My timing is perfect I know just when, so let Me handle the pace"
"This is not a sprint my daughter this is a marathon race"
"So occupy until I come, keep listening for my cues"
"And if I tell you stay, you stay; and move when I say move"
"Waiting is an art you know, it's skills one MUST acquire"
"And once you've mastered the 'art of wait', just watch it take you higher"

"I wait for the Lord; my soul does wait. And in His Word do I hope" (Psalm 30:5 [New American Standard Bible])

"Give all your worries and cares to God, for He cares about you" (I Peter 5:7 [New Living Translation])

What's In a Name?

I gave my three girls the same middle name, Niki', in hopes it would keep them close through the years. It is pronounced Nikee' although most pronounce it Nikki. I think it may have worked, because my girls have demonstrated a tremendous amount of closeness and love for one another over the years, truly being there for each other. I would have attributed it all to the fact that they share the same middle name, except; they have shown this same "'got your back'" sort of closeness to their brother; whom, I might add, I would have given the same middle name too, except he was named after his dad. Besides, I don't think he would have had the same appreciation for it. Now that I say it though, it flows well. Michael Niki'. Nah, He wouldn't go for it.

I have seen so many divided families, and I did not want that for my family. I often threatened them with coming back from the grave if they started feuding after I died. For a hot second, they may have believed me, but they're grown now, and that threat doesn't hold water. Since I was a young believer, I have always told Jesus that I wanted us to be a "Family for God". It is that prayer, more than the same middle name, that God has honored, and that has kept them close. I may be mistaken, but I don't even remember them having an argument among themselves.

Their disagreements, though very few, always seem to lead to what's best to do until they can come to an agreement.

In writing this "What's in A Name" piece, I decided to look up their middle name. I've searched out their first names before but never thought to look up the meaning of the middle name. Niki' means, "People of Victory." How about that? I was so pleased to know it meant something wonderful. At the time that I named them Niki', it was because I liked the way it sounded, not because of its meaning. I knew nothing about names having a meaning when I was naming my babies. But God blessed in spite of my ignorance. Thank You, Daddy.

Young moms, it is so important that you give your child a name conducive to the future you want for them. You don't want to call them something negative day in and day out. The words of our mouth are a testimony and it plants seeds; good or bad. Here are some examples of names that can be construed as having negativity attached to them.

- Cecilia — blind.
- Claudia – lame.
- Deirdre – sorrowful.
- Emily – rival.
- Kennedy – misshapen head.
- Leah — weary.
- Lola – lady of sorrows.
- Mallory – unlucky.
- Mara – bitter

- Wanda - wanderer
- Porchia – pig
- Byron – barn for cows
- Calvin – bald
- Cameron – crooked nose

Those are just a few names with negative origins that some of us may already have. Could it be that our names have kept us back and made it more difficult for us to advance? Would our lives have been any easier with a different name? Who can really say since so many other things contribute to making us the people we have become?

If you have a name with a negative meaning, don't fret. Christ makes the difference in our lives and can make a positive out of any negative that may have followed you through life. He will not hold your name against you just like He doesn't hold your sins against you. But I truly imagine that if some of us have names with negative meanings, God does not use that name when He addresses us. But instead, calls us by our real names—names He has assigned to us. Once our life changes and we began to walk after His ways, He changes our name like He did for Jacob, the supplanter. He calls us by what we now are, not by what we used to be. God can't lie. To call you by a negative name would be a lie. Ask God what your new name is and be addressed by it if possible.

What's in a name? A lot hinges on what thing you are called day in and day out of your life. Those of you who have the chance, give your children a good start in life by naming them something positive. Name them what you want their future to look like. It can only help. I'm so grateful to God for allowing me to accidentally name my girls Niki', "People of Victory." That tradition has continued on to two of my granddaughters, whose middle names are also Niki'.

When God changed a name, it was usually to establish a new identity. I may be changing my name soon. I have a list of possibilities. I realize it will be hard at this juncture in my life. But I want to be called by the destiny that I'm moving toward even if it is late in the game. I believe it was late for Abram and Sarai. They were old when God changed their names to Abraham and Sarah, also. But God did it anyway. And Jacob the *supplanter*, was no spring chicken either when God changed his name to Israel, *Triumphant with God*. The lesson for us is that it is never too late to find your identity in who God made you to be and to ask Him for a name that reflects your true destiny. Whatever your name, remember that the most important name is the name of our Lord, Jesus Christ. His is the name to which every knee will bow and every tongue will confess. Your identity is in Him!

> *"And he said your name shall no longer be called Jacob, but Israel; for you have struggled with God and with men, and have prevailed" (Genesis 32:28 [New King James Version])*

"No longer shall your name be called Abram, but your name shall be called Abraham; For I have made you a father of many nations" Genesis 17:5 [NKJV])

"Then God said to Abraham, as for Sarai your wife, you shall not call her name Sarai, but Sarah shall be her name" (Genesis 17:15 [NKJV])

"Wherefore God also hath highly exalted Him, and given Him the name which is above every name: That at the name of Jesus every knee should bow, of things in heaven, and things in earth, and things under the earth; And that every tongue should confess that Jesus Christ is Lord, to the glory of God the Father" (Philippians 2:9-11 [King James Version])

Deep Wounds

There are things in this life that cause us painfully Deep Wounds. Things that blindside us. You're going along, doing life, and out of nowhere, boom! You're hit with the death of a child, a parent, or a beloved friend. The partner you thought you'd grow old and die with, is abandoning you and wants a divorce. The business partner you trusted and relied on has embezzled the company money and your company is going under. Today you're feeling fine, tomorrow you're diagnosed with a terminal disease. These are all deep wounds. The most important thing to remember about Deep Wounds is that although deep, they are not permanent, though it may feel so at the time of the injury or assault. Time is a very crucial factor in the healing of Deep Wounds. I feel that the Psalmist in the passage below felt the type of pain that Deep Wounds may cause.

"He heals the broken hearted and binds up their wounds" (Psalm 147:3 [New International Version])

There are wounds that can be stitched up and the healing process will begin to take place almost immediately. A daughter you thought was saving herself for marriage is pregnant. This disappointment can require only stitches because the baby, the newest member of your tribe, helps to ease the pain of your wound.

You discover your husband has a porn addiction. This pain may only require stitches if he repents and agrees to go to counseling. Together, you get to the root of his sin. The treatment heals him and he goes on to becomes the man God has called him to be.

Of course, these are just examples and each case is different for each person. Because we are all different with different tolerances and propensities. What's a stitch to one person could very well be a Deep Wound to another.

> *"He lifted me out of the slimy pit, out of the mud and mire; he set my feet on a rock and gave me a firm place to stand" (Ps 40:2 [NIV]).*

There is a broken heart syndrome (BHS) that is real and physical. BHS is a group of symptoms similar to those of a heart attack, occurring in response to emotional stress. Symptoms include; angina or chest pain, shortness of breath, arrhythmia, cardiac shock, fainting, low blood pressure, and heart failure. However, those with BHS do not have blocked arteries and usually make a fast to moderate full recovery. But not always. Some have gone on to need actual open- heart surgery due to the emotional stress BHS has put on their hearts.

Physical pain and emotional pain share the same neural pathways; they both activate the same part of the brain. Research has found that people with BHS who took over the counter Tylenol for three weeks experienced less pain than those who took a placebo.

Yet there are those who experience wounds so deep, they require a process called granulation. Granulation is a process by which the wound is left open, but not uncovered. New connective tissue grows and fills in the wound, starting from the base of the wound.

These wounds are packed and filled in with gauze saturated with medication that promotes healing. This is a slow healing process for wounds that are usually too large to stitch. Daily, and even two to three times a day, the wound needs to be cleaned and the dressings changed.

This is exactly what Jesus did for me when I thought my heart was broken beyond repair. He said, "Run to ME". I did. And He washed and cleansed my deep wounds daily. two, three, four, and sometimes five times a day, He would pack my wounds with His Word, His love, declarations, promises, and hope. Even when I would get tired because it seemed that the wound would never heal, He would beckon me back to Him. He'd say, "sit here and let Me finish treating your wounds". With so much compassion, comfort, and care, He would continue to pack in more of His Word, His love, His promises, and His hope. Until one day I looked up, and my wounds were completely granulated. He is a patient healer. Despite all the pain my Deep Wounds caused, I was saved from brokenness and my heart has been healed.

> *"Though you have made me see troubles, many and bitter, you will restore my life again; from the depths of the earth you will again bring me up"* (Ps 71:20 [NIV]).

God has promised to see His children through any hurtful situation, no matter how painful it may be. He is not a man that He should lie. The thing that we must never forget is that even when it seems we are going through the heartbreak of a Deep Wound, alone; we are never alone. Jesus is trying day by day to get our attention off our pain and focused on the Father. And yet, He understands our despondency and patiently waits for us to give Him our attention so He can guide us to healing. He never gives up on us although we so often give up on ourselves. He understands that although treatment is needed immediately, the healing itself takes time. To rush through the healing process would be like putting a band aide over a bullet wound. And so, He takes His time and sees our healing through to completion.

There will be a scar. Never you mind the scar. It is just a battle scar and serves as a reminder of the battle Jesus fought and won for you.

> *"Weeping may endure for a night, but joy comes in the morning".* (Psalm 30:5b [King James Version])

Section Two

Surely Your goodness and
Unfailing love will pursue me
All the days of my life,
And I will live in the house of the Lord
Forever.
Pslam 23:6 New Living Translation

THE CALL

Many are called but few choose to be chosen

I'm So Pregnant

I'm so pregnant with this thing within me. I can feel it growing more and more each day. It's no longer at a stage of dormant content, when no one knows it's there but You and me.

I'm so pregnant with this thing within me. And it won't be still anymore. It's moving me, stretching me, changing my shape. As it searches for an open door.

I'm so pregnant with this thing within me. It's moving toward an expected end. If I don't deliver this download within me, this baby will die within.

My third trimester is fast approaching, my delivery date is near. Will I bring forth what You've put inside me, or abort this full-term child in fear?

It's run out of room, there is not enough space. It needs freedom from confinement in this tight tiny place. There are those that need to hear what it has to say. There are those who anxiously await its delivery day.

I am pregnant. It's Your Word that's in me. Creations, ideas, and discoveries not made. You are the One Who birthed them within me. So help me dear Lord to not be afraid.

My delivery date has come and gone, the baby's still there, it hasn't been born. You tell me to push the baby's head You can see. But fear, doubt, and shame has its grip on me.

But I hesitate, I ponder, and I wait. The door is quickly closing still I procrastinate. To my doubts and my fears, I am a slave. And my creative womb has become a spiritual grave.

To the creations and ideas You've placed in my heart. To the plans and the businesses You've told me to start. It's not for me that I'll do these things. But to God be the glory and for Jesus my King.

So I ask You Lord for just one more chance. I'll keep my eyes focused I won't even glance; In the direction of doubt that keeps calling my name. I'm done with fear and I'm finished with shame.

By faith I'll be what You've called me to be. I'll push out this baby, I'll set this child free. I am the called and I trust in You, to bring forth this baby. Thank You Jesus, Thank You.

> *"He who received five talents went at once and traded with them, and made five talents more. So also he who had two talents made two talents more. But he who had received the one talent went and dug in the ground and hid his master's money" (Matthew 25:16-18 English Standard Version])*

"And He hath filled him with the Spirit of God, in wisdom, in understanding, and in knowledge, and all manner of workmanship" (Exodus 35:31 [King James Version])

"To these four young men God gave understanding of all kinds of literature and learning. And Daniel could understand visions and dreams of all kinds" (Daniel 1:17 [KJV])

Ten Virgins

There were ten virgins five foolish, five wise
They had just one focus we'll all get inside
They each brought their lamps. They filled them with oil
They're lives had been sprinkled with nutrient rich soil

With gladness they all worked with the kingdom at heart
No one could mislead them from doing their part
Five took their lamps and did barely what they could
Five others took their lamps and did just what they should

The Bridegroom has gone to His home with His friends
The five foolish said "let's get a little play time in"
When we hear the procession come riding down the street
That's when we'll get ready our Savior to greet

How will you be certain you won't miss His call
If your focus is elsewhere you might surely fall
You bear the name Christian but take a look in the mirror
You have some resemblance but you need to draw nearer

For something is missing from the life that you're claiming
It's for your love and your heart and your trust that He's aiming
You five have been warned keep your eyes on the Prize
So when the door finally opens you can say 'still I rise'

We wise look for Him and love his appearing
We expect to see Him soon as the time is nearing
Our lamps are still burning and so are yours
Hope we all will be ready when He throws open those doors

Though the Bridegroom did tarry and took long to return
The five wise kept their focus and showed true concern
By watching and praying and encouraging each other
By lifting through love, never failing to cover

Then the cry came at midnight, "the Bridegroom is on His way!"
"Come yea out to meet Him for tonight is the day"
Then the ten woke from sleeping and took hold of their lamps
They'd been anxiously waiting to break free of this camp

So they jumped to their feet, their lamps to trim
For the five foolish virgins things began to look grim
Their lamps had gone out no extra oil did they bring
It's too late for praying there's no worship songs to sing

Give us of your oil they said in urgent despair
Our lamps have gone out, give us oil if you care
The wise replied No! Then we won't have enough
Why didn't you bring extra when you packed all your stuff

Now you must run to the sellers. Make haste
Go quickly. Don't tarry. Time is precious. Don't waste.
Not a moment, not a minute, not a second my friend
Cause when that door swings open only those ready
will go in

So they ran to the sellers as fast as they could run
But while they were traveling the Bridegroom did come
The five wise that were ready went into the wedding
The five foolish came running and panting and sweating

Please open to us dear Lord we are here
Our lamps are now trimmed and we want to draw near
You five were careless now the door is shut tight
I never knew you, and today has become your night

> *"Watch therefore, for ye know neither the day nor the hour wherein the Son of man cometh" (Matthew 25:13 [King James Version])*

God Cares

I looked out my window and all I could see was blatant disappointment looking back at me.
I tiptoed to the back door and it was there too. I cried out in anguish, Lord what must I do?
I cried and I prayed. I prayed and I cried. I ask You to help me I hurt so inside.
You said that You'd be there never leave or forsake me
You said chains would be broken and I would be set free
God's Answer:
Do you not hear Me whispering sweet things in your ear?
Stroking you with My grace telling you not to fear.
I watch as you struggle, I look down at you and smile.
My peace I left with you so calm down my child.
Do you trust what I told you so long, long ago?
Just be still and listen and let My words flow.
The message from My heart to yours will be clear.
But with your heart you must listen in order to hear.

"So do not throw away this confident trust in the Lord. Remember the great reward it brings you" (Hebrews 10:35 [New Living Translation])

"Do not be anxious about anything, but in everything by prayer and supplication with thanksgiving let your request be made known to God" (Philippians 4:6 [English Standard Version])

God Is in the People Business

You say you can't stand *people*, they get on your nerve
So, tell me my friend, then how will you serve
Cause *people* are the business that Jesus is in
He suffered, bled, and died to save *people* from sin

You steal from the kingdom when you isolate yourself
Take your God-given calling and set it on a shelf
You hide and protect it and keep it all safe
Forgetting that your calling was given by grace

Those *people* your calling was put here to help
Are missing that gift that you've placed on the shelf
Now humble your heart and walk through that door
Stop denying the *people* your gift was sent for

You delay your purpose when you chose procrastination
You steal from the body when you decline participation
Don't bury your talent hiding it safely in the ground
Put your offering on display that your gift may be found

Steward well the gift given, multiply it by sharing
Making sure those who need it may access it through caring
Keep pouring it out and He'll fill up your cup
To further His plan and lift *people* up

God is in the business of making ***people*** brand new
He put His spirit inside so He could partner with you
His command to His children was occupy til I come
That through your faithful obedience you may win someone

God made us one body, we all need each other
Created with purpose to help one another
God is in the business of saving ***people*** from sin
Yes, ***people*** is the business that Jesus is in

> *"For God so loved the world that He gave His only Son That whosoever believes in Him will have everlasting life" (John 3:16 [King James Version])*

> *"For the gifts and callings are without repentance" (Romans 11:29 [KJV])*

Silent Witness

The life you live
The love you give
The things you share
The way you care
The laughter they hear
Your push through fear
The gentleness you show
You never letting go
You Are A Silent Witness

> *"Let your light so shine before men, that they may see your good works and glorify your Father which is in heaven" Matthew 5:16 [King James Version])*

God Is Not Out to Get You

God will chase you down to bless you. He will call you out by name.
He knows who you are, not deterred by your past, He loves you just the same
He'll search for His beloved in the lowest of places to pull you up and out
He'll pursue you to the ends of the earth. That's what love is all about

No condemnation to those of you who are now called by His name
He sees you in the secret places, the places that cause you shame
He says, come out I see you My child, nothing is hidden from My face
He's waiting for you to make a decision to turn and leave that place

Others call you a disgrace and a burden. They hang you out to dry
He says you are the one I died for, the apple of My eye
So don't trip, when in life you stumble, and can't seem to find your way
He says I'm still pursuing you, and I'm just a prayer away

God does not save you by the deeds right or wrong that you do
He's searching your life to see can He see, the Jesus He placed in you
So let Him shine His light in your heart to see what He can see
God is not out to get you...then again...Or Is He?

> *"So you should look for the Lord before it's too late. You should call him now, while He is near" (Isaiah 55:6 [Easy to-Read Version])*

The F-ing Truth

Frankly the feelings of frustration that cause you to fail, fall, faint or fly off the handle
Are based on and factored around few famished folk who force you into fear based on their flimsy facts
You, fearing to forge forward with the food of freedom that has fed your famine.
Folks who are fakers filled with false fruit hurriedly following after false feet
Feuding with family filled with fake fables.
Fans flocking fast to fabricated fame that will fade
Fire flakes falling on fools that flew to the front too fast
Flagrantly fanning the flames of the fire that fuels the festering wound
Fishing for flunkies that will fight for the right to be first to take flack for the fun of being famous
Falling head-first on the fate of the few fat Friday fads
Trying not to be a failure; fly on your face, fawn without fur, fox in the fog, five faux fabrics
Funky, flimsy, freaky, foggy minds, forgetting to be fruitful, faithful, flock feeding, forward facing, forever forgiving, Father followers.
Face your fears, feed your faith, and flow fluidly forward to victory.

Failure is an event, not an identity. Get up, dust yourself off, and continue in the fight!!!

FOCUS! FOCUS! FOCUS!

Growing

Like a brand new plant that's been laying
dormant for a long time
I began shooting up through the dirt
Pushing the dirt from my eyes, I can see the light.
I reach for the sun. It warms my face.
Showers of Your grace
flood the roots of my foundation
which is built upon the Rock
I am Growing

"Like newborn babies, crave pure spiritual milk, So that by it you may grow up in your salvation" (I Peter 2:2 [New International Version])

Not Stunted, Just Delayed

Oh Dear God, here we go again with the stretching and the pulling
Contort my mind, my spirit, and my soul. Until it's shaped just like You need it
I resist and like a rubber band snap back into my place of comfort and familiarity
You try to feed me what is bold and new and fresh from Your treasure of abundance
I take a little on the tip of my tongue and say it's too hot, let me cool it first
I blow and blow and blow and blow until it's cold not cool then I stop

Growing pains don't feel good I say. But You say they're necessary nevertheless
Unused spiritual muscles will be put to work to help shoulder the load that I'll carry
I cringe at the thought. I want to grow but I don't want the pain that comes with it
Can't we be like footprints in the sand, I won't mind if You carry me through it
I carry you when you need to be carried You say. Right now is not the time You say
Take a deep breath and let the growing begin. You're not stunted, just delayed

If it doesn't challenge you, it won't change you

> *"Being confident of this very thing, that He Who begun a good work in you will complete it until the day of Jesus Christ" (Philippians 1:6 [King James Version])*

> *"When I was a child, I spoke and thought and reasoned as a child. When I grew up I put away childish things" (I Corinthians 13:11 [New Living Translation])*

She Came

The first time *she came*, she offered Jesus her life
The second time *she came*, she offered Him the best from her closet
The dress *she came* in was short, tight, flashy, and revealing
Then *she came* up against...The sAints
She came in looking for freedom
She came out feeling judged
She came never again

> *"Don't pick on people, jump on their failures, criticize their faults – unless, of course you want the same treatment. The critical spirit has a way of boomeranging" (Matthew 7:1-2 [Message Bible])*

> *"Scripture: The Lord hath appeared of old unto me, saying, Yea, I have loved thee with an everlasting love: therefore with loving kindness have I drawn thee" (Jeremiah 31:3 [King James Version])*

> *"Judge not that you be not judged. For with what judgement you judge, you will be judged and with what measure you mete, it will be measured to you again" (Matthew 7: 1-2 [KJV])*

"Then the master said to the servant, Go out into the highway and hedges, and compel them to come in, that my house may be filled" (Luke 14:23 [KJV])
A Church Without The Broken Is A Broken Church

The Church Has Left the Building

There's a whole wide world outside that's been waiting on your call.
There's a whole wide world outside these walls about to take a fall
So go outside don't let these walls pretend to hold you in
There's a whole wide world that needs to know there's freedom from their sin

Each time you walk outside the door in case you didn't know
The church has left the building because that church is you, so Go
Evangelize, and prophecy, do great wonders in His name
When you depart they'll know you've been there cause they won't be the same

You are the church and every time you open your mouth to speak
Remember Who you represent, your Savior is meek not weak
So be wise as the subtle serpent yet harmless as the gentle dove
Recalling that your Savior drew them in with kindness and love

The world is falling fast and the answer is in God's word
If the church stays in the building how will His solution ever be heard
We gather every Sunday to get filled and fat and full
And then go home and gather more till our hearing becomes dull

The word should be like dunamis, fire shut up in your bones
A message that you can't contain, that won't leave you alone
It's like a controlled uncontrol burn that's there to manage the weeds
Temperature control by Holy Spirit, set ablaze to meet everyone's needs

If you're looking for the church inside these fancy buildings you see
Just know that's just brick and mortar where we gather every week
It's way past time for the church to step outside of its four walls.
To do what it's been commissioned to do, by answering the Master's call

Come in to worship, depart to serve, and take with you all you can.
God has been waiting for us to leave the building and join Him in His work. ***We are the church.***

> *"Go ye into all the world and preach the gospel to every creature" (Mark 16:15 [King James Version])*

I Just Have To Be Available

I don't have to be emotional
I don't have to be exceptional
I don't have to be sensational
I just have to be available

I don't have to be rich
I don't have to be famous
I don't have to be a star
I just have to be available

I don't have to be organized
Or have it all together
I don't have to be smart
I just have to be available

I don't have to be first
Doesn't matter if I'm last
My past won't hinder me
I just have to be available

Ready when He calls
Following His plan
Staying in my lane
Making myself available

"And I heard the voice of the Lord saying, "Whom shall I send, and who will go for us?" Then I said, "Here am I! Send me" (Isaiah 6:8 [King James Version])

The Grand Canyon Lightbulb Moment

There was once a car, a motorcycle and a bus that decided to engage in a race just for bragging rights. Besides being beautiful to behold, the Hennessey Venom F5 had a top speed of 301 mph with a 1,200-horsepower motor. Its engine was made of billet aluminum with steel cylinder sleeves. The Venom F5 carried a starting price of $1.6 million with up to $600,000 worth in options.

The Dodge Tomahawk motorcycle was a fine specimen of a machine. It was capable of speeds of up to 420 mph and had a 500-horsepower motor with four wheels for added speed. Its body was made of billet aluminum. The rear-wheel drive used monocoque construction. It was an awesome sounding machine when revved up. The going price was $550,000.

A jet powered school bus named "School Time" by its owner can roll out at speeds up to 367 MPH. The school bus was made of steel. School Time, though big and bulky, won many races against vehicles smaller and much lighter than itself. The jet engine gave it an advantage allowing it to take on the challenge of Hennessey Venom and Dodge Tomahawk. The least it could do was come in 2nd. After all, it had a faster speed than Venom. Oh yeah, and despite its name, no children were allowed aboard this school bus.

The thing that made this race extra challenging was the course it would take. It was designed to test who would be first to make it from one side of the Grand Canyon to the other.

Which one would you bet on to make it across? Right! Lightbulb moment. No one would make a wager because the problem is not one of speed. It's one of capability. The gap from one side to the other is much too wide. So, it doesn't matter how fast a vehicle can go.

Similarly, the gap between God and man is wide, and no man can fill it. For centuries, God has been telling us that the work of redemption and salvation is complete. Jesus filled the gap between God and man. So, no amount of money, beauty, prestige, influence, talent, popularity, or any such thing is needed to bridge that gap. None of those attributes will bring you salvation or get you to heaven. So whether you are a Hennessey Venom F5 with all your earthly monetary worth and so many options you can't contain them all; or whether you're a Dodge Tomahawk, with all your beauty and so much power that you have the world at your fingertips; or whether you're "School Time," a jet disguised as a bus; When you get to the edge of the Grand Canyon, you will get a rude awakening. If the lightbulb fails to come on for you, you will find yourself plunging toward certain death. It doesn't matter what skin you're in down here. From the White House to the poor house, we must all come to God the same way: through Jesus. Jesus was sent to bridge the gap. He died in our place, so we would not have to die. Don't let your lightbulb moment come too late.

> *"For God so loved the world that He gave His only begotten Son, that whosoever believeth in Him should not perish but have everlasting life" (John 3:16 [King James Version])*

> *"The Lord is not slack concerning His promises, as some men count slackness, but is longsuffering to us, not willing that any should perish, but that all should come to repentance" (II Peter 3: 9 [KJV])*

Stood Up

(a monologue pt. I)

A woman is pacing nervously back and forth looking at her watch. Bible is sitting on the table where she normally has her "quiet time" with God. Finally, when she can't take it any longer:

Lord, where are You? You're always here. It's 6 am. You're never late. You're always here for me. I know it's been about 2 weeks. Well... 2 and a half weeks since I've met You here, but I've been soooo busy. I really have tried to meet with You. At my job, they're working me like a Hebrew slave. I know You can relate to that Lord. I'm exhausted when I finally get home. God forbid it's a church night. By the time I get home, I can barely drag myself into bed. I mean, You know. You've caught me sleeping on my knees before.

(searching for God even more anxiously)

Lord, where are you? I've got so much to tell You. So much has happened since I was last here. It hasn't all been great either. I need to tell You about the good, the bad, and the ugly. And I do mean ugly.

Oh God, it's 6:05 where are You?

I want to share some good news with You. I have a brand-new grandson who was born last week. His name is Israel. He weighed 8lbs 1.4oz. and has 10 fingers and 10 toes. He has the cutest little button nose and all his parts are working properly. He's perfect. You did good God, and I just want to thank You. Thank You that he and his mom came through the delivery safe and sound. Thank You for sending Your angels to watch over them both.

I need to talk to You about the bad too, Lord. My son was supposed to meet me for lunch the other day and he stood me up again. That hurt so bad, Lord. I must have cried for the rest of the day every time I thought about it. I wanted to tell him face to face how much I love him. How I wish I could take him in my arms like I did when he was little, hold him, protect him, and make things alright again. He is so distant, Lord. He wants nothing to do with his dad and me. He's living outside of Your protection. I need You to protect him until he's back inside Your safety zone—under Your blood. Oh God, where are You? This thing can't wait.

I especially want to tell you about the ugly, Lord. You know I love Your people with all my heart, but I declare, sometimes they are so hard to get along with. They will twist a person's words up and have me saying stuff I never said. Like last week, when I told my dear sister that I had some advice for her on how she could better run the "Helping Hands" ministry. You know, some tips on how to make it run smoother? Well, this sister got all bent out of shape, got an attitude, said I was trying to run her department and has all but stopped talking to me. I didn't mean for it to sound like I was trying to boss her. I don't want to be the boss of nobody! I have a hard enough time keeping me straight. And besides, I know that those ideas for the ministry came from You.

Lord, it's 6:15. You are never late. Never! Where are You???

God's Response: (pt. II)

My child, My child, I'm right here. I've always been here. You're having a hard time sensing My presence because you've been so busy and distracted lately. I haven't been able to reach you through My Word, because it's been quite some time now since you've picked up your Bible. Our line of communication has been broken. I feel "*stood up*." You know, "*stood up*." Like when you're expecting someone to pick you up for a date and they never show. Like when you waited on your son, and he never came?

I wait for you every morning, and when you don't show up, I miss you. I long to hear you call My name. I miss the supplication and prayers that you sent Me in times past. I miss the adoration you give, and I miss bathing you in the morning dew of My love. I miss speaking to you in My still small voice. I miss our communion together.

And don't worry, I'm very much aware of the good, the bad, and the ugly. I see it all. I would never leave you alone in those dark times. But if you neglect our times together, and our line of communication is broken, I will be right there, but you won't know it. I'm Your Heavenly Father, and My desire is to take care of you in every aspect of your life. But, in order for Me to do that, you must lay up treasures in heaven where moth and rust cannot corrupt. For where your treasure is, there your heart will be also. Mathew 6:19-20.

Please don't neglect our time together. Our relationship is valuable to Me. Does it hold value for you, My child?

ME: Yes Lord, it does. Forgive me for Standing You up. Our relationship is important to me. It's very important to me.

GOD: I forgive you, My Child.

ME: Thank You, Lord. See You in the morning.

> *"Come close to God and He will come close to you" (James 4:8a [New Living Translation])*

> *"The Lord is near to all who call on Him, to all who call on Him in truth" (Psalm 145:18 [King James Version])*

> *"Then Jesus told His disciples a parable to show them that they should always pray and not give up" (Luke 18:1 [New International Version])*

Section Three

In Your strength I can crush an army;
With my God I can scale any wall.
Psalm 18:29 New Living Translation

THE BATTLES WE FIGHT

I don't know but I been told, Jesus Christ can make you bold

(said to the tune of an army cadence)

2020 Vision

It's too late satan I know too much
you should have killed me when you had the chance
My knowledge base is much too wide
And my wisdom is much too advanced

My vision is so much clearer now
Much clearer than when we first met
I've got 2020 vision on all four sides
I've got Jesus as my safety net

The weapons I use are not carnal
The eyes I see with are not my own
The ears that I use to hear your lies
Sit high upon God's throne

So before you come attacking me
Let's get this one thing clear
This is one battle you will not win
2020 is not your year

> "Then Elisha prayed and said, O Lord, I pray, open his eyes that he may see. And the Lord opened the servant's eyes and he saw; and behold the mountain was full of horses and chariots of fire all around Elisha" (II Kings 6:17 [New American Standard Bible])

Run Toward Your Fear

On your mark, get set, run toward your fear
If the task is from God, then HE'LL meet you there
Join HIM where HE'S working so you will succeed
Outside of HIS will there are no guarantees

Don't let the size of the task paralyze you
Customized by the Master to fit a size 'You two'
If it's bigger than you then you know it's from HIM
If you can do it alone, pray about it again

Let's not be like Jonah and try to escape
J M told you to just "do it afraid"
Don't turn your back, don't run from the LORD
Yours won't be a whale but for sure will be hard

The assignment is not something that you cannot do
But you'll need HIS help to see this thing through
So don't embrace fear when it knocks at your door
Open the door wide and shout, "I Trust In The Lord!"

One more time my friend, let me make myself clear
Don't worry about your future, God is already there
Keep moving forward though sometimes you can't see
He's the fear extinguisher, clearing your path of all debris

On your mark, get set, run toward your fear
Let that fear know that JESUS is here
Let fear know it was conquered that day on the cross
Today you have victory, today fear has lost

> *"For God did not give us a spirit of fear (timidity), but of power and love and sound judgement" (II Timothy 1:7 [New Living Translation/Christian Standard Bible])*

Rhu

Running after God, with all my strength and might
Sometimes the things I'm reaching for seem far and out of sight
But God says just keep striving cause I've called you for this day
When things seem like they won't work out, stop, seek My face and pray

So don't stop running, don't slow down, keep your goals in sight
It's not the speed that you run, push on through darkest night
Keep your eyes on the prize, no looking back, focus on the race
And trust the one who assigned you the task to help you keep the pace

You will encounter naysayers that will try to slow you down
Look them straight in the eye, set your face like a flint, and say I'm heaven bound
So what I'm saying baby girl is keep your eyes on things above
Don't stop till you've done all He's given you to do. And do it all in love.

"Wherefore the rather, brethren, give diligence to make your calling an election sure: for if you do these things, you will never fall" (II Peter 1:10 [King James Version])

Every Truth Don't Have to Be Told

Just because you know a thing,
Don't mean you have to say that thing
Even if that thing is true
What good would it do
For you to open your mouth and assassinate a person
Now they're a corpse and you're a murderer
No one wins, everyone hurts
Hold your peace so there can be peace
Every Truth Don't Have To Be Told

> *"Let your conversation be always full of grace, seasoned with salt, so that you may know how to answer everyone" (Colossians 4:6 [English Standard])*

> *"Sin is not ended by multiplying words, but the prudent hold their tongue" (Proverbs 10:19 [New International Version])*

> *"The soothing tongue is a tree of life, but a perverse tongue crushes the spirit" (Proverbs 15:4 [NIV])*

The Victory Is In Your Mouth

Open your mouth and speak it
It's as close as the breath you breathe
Say out loud that thing you need
The answer you seek is in Me

Call those things that be not yet
As though they were already here
Say those things you dare not say
Speak them out loud and clear

If it's healing that you need right now
Say by His stripes I'm healed
Believe by faith, not what you see
And victory will be revealed

The atmosphere is waiting
To hear your faith filled decrees
Let your words burst through with power
He's waiting to meet every need

Son or daughter gone astray
Giving up is not an option
You taught them what was right from wrong
The words you declare can block them

Your marriage seems to be failing
It seems though this is the end
It's not just what you do that heals
Your words can restore and transcend

Talk to God and say restoration is so
Speak peace in your home today
Say about your marriage what God says is true
Open your mouth speak His Word and obey

I think I might get fired you say
What you speak will probably come true
Step up your game and say the right thing
A promotion could be waiting for you

Say what you want not what you don't want
What you say will direct your pursuits
The words you speak are more important than you know
Words spoken from the heart form truths

> *"Death and life are in the power of the tongue"*
> *(Proverbs 18:21 [King James Version])*

> *"For out of the abundance of the heart the mouth speaks" (Matthew 12:34 [KJV])*

Between Your Head and Your Heart Lies Your Mouth

If the words that want to come from your mouth
Are not helpful, good, pure, and encouraging,
Lock them up!
Do not let them escape!
Like a prisoner on lock down,
Keep them under lock and key!
For your words reveal your heart.

"For out of the abundance of the heart the mouth speaks" (Matthew 12:34b [King James Version])

"Let the words of my mouth and the meditation of my heart, be acceptable in Thy sight, O Lord my strength and my redeemer" (Psalm 19:14 [King James Version])

The Art of Waiting

Waiting is an art. Yes, the art of waiting takes on a life of its own.
It is the plains between the mountains and the valleys
It is the dash between the beginning and the end
It is the space between now and then
Waiting is not to be wasted on nothingness

What you do while you wait is of the utmost importance
So while waiting, we must kill it's enemy, procrastination
Procrastination is an enemy of doing and a murderer of time
Give it all you got, to do all you can, to make the wait worthwhile

Waiting is an art. The art of waiting takes on a life of its own
It is the years between birth and death
It is the try harder between first and last
It is that place between here and there
Waiting is not to be wasted on nothingness

Waiting well means this time keep going
Even if you can't see the end of the tunnel
You know that every beginning has an end
In this life nothing last forever, yet forever is your goal

Waiting is an art. The art of waiting takes on a life of its own
It is the span between infancy and old age
It is the pause between stop and start
It is the vision between clarity and blurriness
Waiting is not to be wasted on nothingness

The art of waiting is being able to rest
All the while when you're going through
It's allowing the orchestra conductor to change the song
Just when you got the rhythm right in your head

Waiting is an art. The art of waiting takes on a life of its own
It is the pain between a lie and the truth
It is the nine months between conception and birth
It is the anticipation between "will you marry me" and "I do"
Waiting is not to be wasted on nothingness

It's the ballerina that practices and practices
Until her toes are raw and sore
Then finds out on the night of her performance
That she was to dance to Nutcracker instead of Swan Lake

Waiting is an art. The art of waiting takes on a life of its own
It is the decision between right and wrong
It is the gavel between freedom and imprisonment
It is the atom between light and darkness
Waiting is not to be wasted on nothingness

Waiting is gaining control while losing control all at the same time
It is the short thin line between love and hate
It is taking hold while also letting go
It is giving in while never ever giving up
The art of waiting takes on a whole new life as we place it in the Artist's hands

> *"Wait for the Lord: Be strong and let your heart take courage. wait for the Lord" (Psalm 27:14 [English Standard Version])*

> *"Rest in the Lord and wait patiently for Him. Do not fret because of him who prospers in his way" (Psalm 37:7 [New American Standard Bible])*

> *"I will wait for the Lord, my soul waits, and in His word I hope" (Psalm 130:5 [ESV])*

> *"Lead me in your truth and teach me, for You are the God of my salvation; For You I wait all the day" (Psalm 25:5 [NASB])*

A Roar Too Loud to Ignore

It used to be that you had to stop and think
Was that an attack by the enemy?
But now it's a new day and before you can blink
I'm all in your face saying "hey look it's me"

I used to be a prowler sneak in from the back
For fear you would catch and rebuke me
But now I come in with full frontal attack
Walk right up to you but you can't see

The laws of the land in the palm of my hand
My roar so loud it's earth shaking
I've twisted and turned it to fit in my plan
I've blinded your eyes with the quaking

I'm invisible yet I am right in plain sight
Cause you chose yourself not to see
I'm roaring so loud and my sin is so bright
I've revved up to the nth degree

You see I no longer have to quietly prowl
I just put a cell phone in your hand
I sit back watch every man, woman, and child
Become mesmerized at my command

Porno at the touch of your fingertips
Child molestation on the rise
Come hither let me get you in my grips
It's free come feast your eyes

I walk in and sit in your living room
By way of your cable TV
I babysit your little children at noon
And rock them to sleep every eve

I sit in high places just as bold as I can
Roaring SAME SEX MARRIAGE OK
But against Christian freedoms I take my stand
Sleep on saints it's a new day

There is no control on gun control
I have vowed to keep it that way
Teens killing classmates with guns they've been sold
Or the guns parents thought they put away

Long gone are the days of prowl and pounce
My sneaking days are over I roared
I showed up here just so I could announce
My roar is too loud to be ignored.

> *"Be sober minded, be alert. Your adversary the devil is prowling around like a roaring lion, looking for anyone he can devour" (I Peter 5:8 [Christian Standard Bible])*

The enemy used to prowl quietly like a lion hunting prey, but his footsteps and his roar are so loud in these last days he can no longer stay hidden. And though he thinks this boldness makes him more powerful, his visibility only makes him more vulnerable.

Brokenness Continuum

Broken boy meets Broken girl
They marry and raise Broken children
Their Broken children meet other Broken children
Because Brokenness attracts Brokenness
They marry and produce Broken grandchildren
Someone PLEASE Break the continuum of Brokenness
Will it be you?

"Seek ye the Lord while He may be found, call ye upon Him while He is near: Let the wicked forsake his way, and the unrighteous man his thoughts: and let him return to the Lord, And He will have mercy upon him; and to our God, for He will abundantly pardon" (Isaiah 55: 6-7 [King James Version])

Distract, Discourage, Destroy

Distraction

The bills are due, your job is calling, the spouse is not happy, the children are acting out, you won't get the raise, the credit card is maxed out, the nursing home is calling because your parents' health is failing, your hair is falling out, depression is starting to invade your emotions, and your friend is upset with you.

Discouragement

I am afraid that we will run out of money, I feel inadequate at work, I don't know what I did wrong, I am worried that my children don't respect me anymore, I don't feel valued, I am afraid of collapse in my personal finances, I'm scared about losing my mom and dad, I'm terrified that I might be seriously ill and I don't feel attractive anymore, I feel like I'm losing my mind, I miss the connection and support of my friends.

Destroy

Gotcha!

When the enemy comes in, **like a flood the Spirit of the Lord will lift up a standard against him**. Isaiah 59:19

When the enemy comes in like a flood, the Spirit of the Lord will lift up a standard against him. Isaiah 59:15

Any way you say it, and wherever you place the comma and emphasis, the enemy is still defeated. He comes to distract by any means necessary. No tactic is too low for him to use. He uses his distractions to discourage you. He knows that once you fall into discouragement from the distractions, destruction is right around the corner.

Keep your armor on at all times. Your defensive armor consists of your helmet, breastplate, shield, and footwear. Most importantly, your only piece of offensive armor is your sword. Learn to use it skillfully slicing the enemy to pieces when he dares come for you. Let him know that you know that distractions are a part of life and you may be attacked by discouragement from time to time. But make certain he knows that "Gotcha," is not an option. You are armed and dangerous and will never be caught without your armor; trusting in God, and leaning not to your own understanding.

> *"Be sober, be vigilant; because your adversary the devil, as a roaring lion, walketh about, seeking whom he may devour" (I Peter 5:8 [King James Version])*

"Trust in the Lord with all your heart; do not depend on your own understanding. Seek His will in all you do, and He will show you which path to take" (Proverbs 3: 5-6 [English Standard Version])

Don't Let This Melanin Fool You

Melanin, or the lack thereof, should not be so great a concern to us since, whatever our outer covering is, it is given to us by the Father and is only a protective covering for the important parts that lie underneath. And since He gave it to you, trust, **He loves the skin you're in**.

I have often wondered how this thinnest and largest organ that we possess can be used to separate us to such a great degree. Inside, we are all the same. And because the body alone is made up of thousands of parts, it is far easier to find more ways we are alike than different. We all have 2 eyes, 2 ears, 1 nose, and 1 mouth to compose our face. We all, (with few exceptions), have 2 arms, 2 legs, and a torso on which to hang them; 10 fingers, 10 toes, 2 feet, 2 elbow joints, 2 knee joints, and that's only a partial list of just the outside. We all need oxygen to breathe and the same red blood runs through all of our veins and arteries. And did you know that a transplanted heart will function with the same accuracy without prejudice regarding the ethnicity of the donor or recipient? That alone speaks volumes. A study from Johns Hopkins Medicine reviewed 20,185 heart transplant patients who had surgery at 140 hospitals. Researchers found that recipients of organs from donors with the same racial background did no better or worse than those who received organs from donors of different races.

God knew what HE was doing when HE made us alike (on the inside), and HE knew what HE was doing when HE made us different (on the outside). Yet, once our outer covering is applied, it seems to change everyone's perspective. One race is deemed superior to the other because of its protective covering? Absolute nonsense!

Interestingly, disaster seems to be the only thing that opens our eyes to our alikeness. In times of crisis, we set aside our differences because we know the truth is that we are better, stronger, and safer together.

> *Hebrews 9:27 tells that we are **all** destined to die once, and after that to face judgement,*

Our differences should instead cause us to be curious about and want to learn of, other people's cultures and ways of life, not destroy them. Why would anyone want to destroy what the Creator has made and called, "Good?" Our God is the Master of creativity and cleverness. It would be so unlike HIM to make us all the same on the outside as well as the inside. How boring. How mundane. How very uninteresting. And God is on the total opposite end of the spectrum when it comes to uninteresting. I conclude that God in HIS sovereign omniscience, made us different for ***our*** pleasure and to keep life interesting while we journey through here to our intended and eternal homeland. He made us alike on the inside so that we would recognize our connectivity to one another. And it doesn't hurt that our parts are exchangeable in an emergency.

I have learned several tidbits from other cultures. But what I cherish most, I have learned from the race that I am the closest associated with. When it comes to music, my Caucasian or white brothers and sisters have taught me the difference between worship and inspirational music. For this, I will forever be grateful. Growing up in the black church, I knew gospel inspirational music well. This is not to say we didn't have worship music, but it was the inspirational music that we mostly embraced. The fast, upbeat music went over better because of our culture, and I believe it was what we needed at the time as an oppressed people. We attended church often and got our dose of inspirational music to help us make it until we met again. Life was pretty hard for most. But inspirational music did just that—inspired you about what God could and would do for you to lift you up and out of your present situation. It did not speak much of who HE really is within Himself, all by Himself, and just because. A lot of it did not speak about what HE had already done that we just needed to grab hold of and believe. Who is God (*to you*), without talking so much about what HE will do (*for you*)? ***Who is HE in all HIS greatness alone that makes HIM worthy to be praised?*** God inhabits the praises of HIS people. ***As we enter into HIS presence, HE enters into our praise.*** That's when we began to see God for Who HE really is. That's when we began to see HIM the way HE wants us to see HIM.

God started my transformation years ago when I visited Dr. Mike Maiden's church. They were still meeting in an airplane hangar. I clearly heard God speak to me and say, "you will attend here for one year." HE had some things HE wanted to show me and teach me, and this was the place. A new light was shed on worship for me during that year with Pastor Maiden. At first, I didn't even know what was different. I just knew that when we sang, it was like my heart was opening up anew. There I learned to slow down and hear Who God was through their songs. I guess you can say. it was the beginning of my worship journey. I said all that to say, God used another culture to teach me what HE wanted me to know about worship. God did not intend our protective covering which I'll call our "***organ protectors***" to cause war between us. **Don't let this melanin or lack thereof in some cases, fool you**; inside we are all the same and in Christ we are equals. We are the body of Christ. Each one with an intricate part and a unique function. So, let us, with all that's within us, work together, love one another, and let us follow God's intended plan.

> *"For by ONE Spirit are we ALL baptized into ONE BODY, whether we be Jews or Gentiles, whether we be bond or free; and have been ALL made to drink into ONE Spirit"* (I Corinthians 12:13 [King James Version])

*"If anyone says, "**I love God**", yet **hates his brother,** he is a liar. For anyone **who** does not **love his brother,** whom he has seen, cannot **love God,** whom he has not seen. And He has given us this command: Whoever loves **God** must also **love his brother**" (I John 4:20 [New International Version])*

False Evidence Appearing Real

We must expose fear for what it really is. There are some things we fear because we expect a certain outcome. For example, during tax season, some may fear that they will have to pay huge tax amounts because they are single, don't have enough tax write offs, or fail to have enough withholdings. Sometimes we fear the consequences of our negative actions will bring negative repercussions. That is a real fear. It is based on cause and effect.

But there are times when we just fear the unknown. We fear fear, and usually anticipate the worst. We don't know the outcome, and it causes anxieties and foreboding. I know this to be true because I have asked God; why can't I just know? Why can't the appointed time be now? He has to remind me time and again that He knows what's best for me. He sees *all*, knows *all*, and is in *every* place at the *same* time.

So, now when the dread of the unknown rears its ugly head, I remind myself that it is False Evidence Appearing Real. I picture Dorothy, Toto, the Tin Man, Cowardly Lion, and Scarecrow hiding and shivering with fear until they go and expose the little bully behind the curtain. Once the curtain is pulled, the wizard becomes a regular 'ole' man. The thing is, he was a regular 'ole' man all the time. He was putting out false evidence so he could appear to be a real wizard. In the same way, our enemy puts out false evidence so threats can appear to be a bigger challenge and opponents can seem scarier than they really are. The most important thing we must remember when coming up against any fear is that the God within us is greater than the forces of this world (I John 4:4). God in us is greater than any fear that could come against us. So, don't *give in to fear, give fear to Jesus. He can handle it.*

> *"Don't fear for I have redeemed you; I have called you by name; you are Mine" (Isaiah 43:1 [King James Version])*

> *"Perfect love cast out all fear" (I John 4:8 [KJV])*

The Verbal Arsonist

I once taught a Sunday school class of preteens where I led them in an experiment to demonstrate the power of the tongue and the damage it can cause if not controlled. I brought tubes of toothpaste to class and gave each child one. I placed newspaper on the table in front of them. I instructed each one to squeeze as much of the toothpaste as they could out of the tube onto the paper. This was the fun part. They went at it full force. I think they may have thought whoever's toothpaste pile was the biggest was the winner. I then offered a dollar to the one who could get the toothpaste back in the tube. They all looked at me as if I were nuts. They, of course, knew without trying that this was an impossible task.

I went on to explain to them that this is how it is when we speak words of hurt to someone. There is no way to "take it back" as we used to say as kids. The damage is done and can often run deep. Hurtful words spoken or heard can sometimes follow you into adulthood and affect the way you relate or fail to relate to people. I'd hoped that that little demonstration would stick with them into adulthood and cause them to think before speaking in anger.

Another similar activity to demonstrate how damaging words spoken out of turn can be is to hand out aluminum foil cut into the shape of a heart. Instruct students to crumple the foil. After a few minutes, ask them to straighten out the foil. The students quickly realized that there is no way to make it flat again. The heart, though still shaped like a heart, would never be the same again.

The power of the tongue cannot be overstated. It has been compared to a serpent, a sword, and a ship's rudder among other things. But the Bible makes a more stark comparison.

Arsonist: one who deliberately sets fires to property.

Verbal Arsonist: one whose tongue is used to intentionally destroy others.

James chapter 3 gives us a description of how unruly the tongue is. James says that the tongue is a fire. Of all the body parts, the tongue, though small, can corrupt the whole body and set the whole course of a life on fire. Just by saying the wrong thing at the wrong time, (or the right time some would say), the verbal arsonist can set a person's life on a path of destruction or cause it to take a downward spiral. Worse still, it can have a domino effect and destroy several lives simultaneously including the life of the speaker.

I hear people say all the time, "I'm just straight forward", or "I just say what I feel." It's ok to be who you are. However, you and I have an obligation to be "wise as serpents" but "harmless as doves." We should always take into consideration the damage and destruction that could be left behind by hurtful words not carefully contemplated before we speak. Sometimes this is just an indication that people do not want to put any restraints on their mouths and use this as an excuse to say anything they want. I'm not being unrealistic to think that we must walk on eggshells. I'm speaking of that person whose tongue-wagging and inconsideration is chronic, not occasional.

James goes on to say, in verse 7, that man has tamed all manner of earthly creatures, but no man can tame the tongue.

More people have been destroyed with the tongue than by rape, incest, and other heinous acts combined. Social media has caused a rise in teen suicide because kids are made to feel worthless, hated, and disliked before thousands, leaving them to feel as if their lives are not worth living. "But it was only words spoken", some may say. "Stick and stones may break my bones, but words will never hurt me," they say. But they are wrong. Words wound, words hurt, and words can kill. Proverbs 17:22 says: A cheerful heart is good medicine, but a crushed spirit dries up the bones.

It only takes a tiny spark to set an entire forest on fire and burn up thousands of acres killing animals and destroying the ecosystem, animal habitats, and homes or businesses. In the same way, your words can trigger an emotional blaze. The words you put into the atmosphere, much like the toothpaste, cannot be taken back and can cause a lifetime of harm.

Some people have a gift of gab, which can be used for good or bad. When used for good, it can bring blessings, comfort, or words of wisdom to the hearer. When used otherwise, it can be a dangerous weapon. It is like being armed with an AK-47 machine gun, leaving your victims riddled with holes and wounds.

So where do repentance, forgiveness, and healing enter the discussion? We are not able to undo the damage we do with our hurtful words. Only Jesus can unscramble scrambled eggs, put the toothpaste back in the tube, and restore the glossy sheet of aluminum. He can bring total healing to hearts wounded by words. But why take the chance of ruining a life that belongs to God or that may someday belong to God. Turn your tongue over to Jesus and let Him sanctify it today. He is the only one that can control this tiny uncontrollable member of our body. ***Don't be a verbal arsonist.***

> *"And the tongue is a fire, a world of iniquity: so is the tongue among our members, that it defiles the whole body, and set on fire the course of nature: and it is set on fire of hell" (James 3:6 [King James Version])*

> *"Set a watch, O Lord, before my mouth; keep the door of my lips" (Psalm 141:3 [KJV])*

Section Four

The heavens proclaim the glory of God.
The skies display His craftmanship.
Day after day they continue to speak;
Night after night they make Him known.
Psalm 19:1-2 NLT

God Is

I blame God for every good thing that happens to me

The Help

Faster than a crushing abandonment
More powerful than a destructive lie
Able to leap fatal disappointments in a single bound
LOOK! Within your heart!
It's the Father,
It's the Son,
It's the Holy Ghost!

"My help comes from the Lord, the Maker of heaven and earth" (Psalm 121:2 [New International Version])

"God will defeat your enemies who attack you. They'll come in at you on one road and run away on seven roads" (Deuteronomy 28:7 [Message Bible])

"For the eyes of the Lord run to and fro throughout the whole earth, to show Himself strong on behalf of those whose heart is loyal to Him" (II Chronicles 16:9 [New King James Version])

God, You Are

God, You Are infinity beyond infinity
You never change and in You is no variableness neither shadow of turning
You are the same yesterday, today, and forever
You are Omnipotent, Omniscient, and Omnipresent
You are the one God and Father of all who is over all and through all in all
You are the First and the Last, the Beginning and the Ending, the Alpha and Omega,
The Author and the Finisher of my faith.
There is none like unto You
You are I Am that I Am
You are the One who knows the stars by name, how many grains of sand are on every beach
The number of hairs on my head
The winds and the waves obey Your will
You are the invisible force against my enemies.
You are my peace in the midst of my storms.
You are the lover of my soul.
You are the joy and the strength of my life
Your Majesty! You Are So Much More Than That!

"Who is the King of glory? The LORD Almighty, He is the King of glory" (Psalm 24:10 [New International Version])

"Who can fathom the Spirit of the LORD, or instruct the LORD as His counselor?" (Isaiah 40:13 [NIV])

Relentless Love

I have never known a love like Yours before. The love You have for Your children is not an ordinary love. It is relentless, unconditional, and everlasting. When the love of others waxes cold, Your love persists. You love us even though You thoroughly know us. I mean—*really* know us. With all of our faults and failures, your love never changes. When we fall into the deepest darkest places, it is an unconditional love that reaches down to pull us up and out. The Bible calls it the miry clay, a pit of destruction. When we are so covered with the mud, clay, and filth of the world that we do not even resemble one of Yours, You continue to beckoning us to You. Then You lift us up, clean us up, and set us on the righteous path. With patient love, you wait and long for an opening, an opportunity to get our attention. Even when we push our lips out, throw our hands up, turn our backs, and walk away, You continue to pursue us. You do not give up on us. Your love keeps calling out to us saying there is room at the cross for you. Our crimes and our sins are ever before You, yet You still say, "Come". You chase us down and tell us that You love us still. You gently remind us that, no matter what the sin, it is covered by the blood of Your Son, Jesus. Your love is *relentless*, and there is nothing that can stop You from coming after Your lost children.

"You will be My people and I will be your God"
(Jeremiah 30:22 [New Living Translation])

If a man has a hundred sheep and one of them wanders away, what will he do? Won't He leave the ninety-nine others on the hills and go out to search for the one that is lost? And if he finds it, I tell you the truth, he will rejoice over it more than over the ninety-nine that didn't wander away! In the same way, it is not my heavenly Father's will that even one of these little ones should perish" (Matthew 18:12 [NLT])

God Speaks Ebonics

Go ahead, say what you gotta say
Speak to God in the language you know
There will be no communication gaps
Every dialect in the earth is in His repertoire
He doesn't just speak Greek and Hebrew
English, Spanish, German, or Chinese
He will communicate with you
In whatever language you speak
Go ahead, add a little slang if you must
He hears you loud and clear
He'll bend His ear close to the earth
Just to hear you call upon His name
He's interested in what you have to say
He's interested in your repentant heart
God speaks Ebonics

"Whoever has My commands and keeps them is the one who loves Me. The one who loves Me will be loved by My Father, and I too will love them and show Myself to them" (John 14:21 [New International Version])

"My command is this: Love each other as I have loved you" (John 15:12 [NIV])

God Understands Rap

Speak to God my rapping brother and my rapping sister.
Let those words roll off your tongue in the beautiful
poetry that you have been blessed to hear in your head.
Let the rhythmic sounds tingle our ears as you run up and
down the grammatical scale in pure articulate fashion.
Give glory to Him with the gift you have been
anointed with.
God understands rap!
He created your abilities, and He loves it!

"Every desirable and beneficial gift comes out of heaven"
(James 1:17 [Message Bible])

No Pumping Necessary

You don't have to pump me to praise my God
I'm already pumped, I'm already primed
God is too good for me to sit on my hands
When I enter His courts I'm ready to praise

I start my day off early in His presence
I try to stay in His presence throughout my day
So if and when the enemy comes at me
I don't stutter when I put him in his place

I don't profess "I'm Going Through"
But I confess "I'm Coming Through"
I praise my Lord for everything
Because without Him who am I anyway

I come through His doors with a praise on my lips
When worship is raised my hands go up
I'm already pumped, I'm already primed
It takes only the mention of His Name

You've tenderized my heart O God
My response to You is immediate
Just to think of Your goodness causes me to shout
The songs remind me of Your faithfulness

You are God and God alone
This my soul knows right well
I will worship You all the day long
I'm already pumped, I'm already primed

> *"Enter into His gates with thanksgiving, and into His courts with praise: Be thankful unto Him and bless His name. For the Lord is good; His mercy is everlasting; and His truth endures to all generations" (Psalm 100:4-5 [King James Version])*

Er-Body Talkin' Bout Goliath

Er-body Talkin' Bout Goliath:

I Samuel 17:4-7 says;
Then Goliath, a Philistine champion from Gath, came out of the Philistine ranks to face the forces of Israel. He was over nine feet tall! He wore a bronze helmet, and his bronze coat of mail weighed 125 pounds. He also wore bronze leg armor, and he carried a bronze javelin on his shoulder. The shaft of his spear was as heavy and thick as a weaver's beam, tipped with an iron spearhead that weighed 15 pounds. His armor bearer walked ahead of him carrying a shield.

The fear of Goliath had filled the camps of the army of the Israelites and they talked of him constantly. "Do you see how this man keeps coming out? He comes out to defy Israel", they say. "The king will give wealth to the man that kills him. He will give him his daughter in marriage and will exempt his family from taxes".

Some of us are like the army of Israel in that we speak constantly about the things that we feel will defeat us, not understanding that it is because of our speech that these things *are* able to defeat us. We magnify our problems and give them power. We put out into the atmosphere what we see instead of what we want to see. It doesn't matter if it's sickness and disease, financial situations, relationship issues, problems on our job or business, or issues with our children. We allow our worries and fears to spill out.

We must not let the conversation of Goliath dominate our speech.

Magnify Him!

David heard what they were saying of Goliath. It never crossed his mind to ask if it was true. He didn't care. David never inquired about Goliath's status. He wasn't interested in his numbers; his height, his weight, how many battles he had won, etc. What he wanted to know was, "Who is this uncircumcised Philistine who dares challenge the army of the Living God?" He knew it wasn't right for anyone to speak against the Almighty God. David was probably thinking, **"Er-Body Talkin' Bout Goliath, Nobody Talkin' Bout God.** Have you all forgotten Who it is we serve? The one and only true God and creator of all the universe. The creator of every living creature, and of the earth that we all reside on. Why are you all speaking about this Goliath like he is greater than our God? I'll fight him!"

What David knew of his God is what he had experienced. David had spent long hours alone with God out in the shepherd's field. David knew God as a warrior and a defender. While his father and brothers looked down on David as a mere sheep tender, the time out in the fields alone afforded him the opportunity to hear from God and experience

Him as a protector. It seemed that David was expendable to his father and his family. Why else would he be sent into the fields alone when there were 7 other sons? Out into a desert where he could be—and was—attacked by lions and bears? No brother could go with him to share the burden? And when all of his brothers were called in to meet the prophet, why was David left behind? They underestimated him because of his size. They did not understand that time with God makes you more powerful than your outward appearance can convey.

Time alone with God:

Time alone with God is an important aspect of every child of God's life. Get this right and you will have conquered half the battle of hearing from God. The other half is practice, practice, practice, and more practice. Practice listening for His voice. Practice comparing it to His word. Practice doing what He says even if you don't always understand the why. Practice doing what He says even if you don't get it right all the time. This is not an exact science. This is a walk of faith, which is better than an exact science because it is guaranteed that if you do what you know to do, He will always do what He's promised to do. In other words, be diligent to put in the time.

Better Than Exact Science:

Take the law of gravity for instance. It is guaranteed that if you jump off a 3-story building you will, in a matter of seconds, hit the ground. THIS IS A GUARANTEE. It doesn't matter if you believe in gravity or not. Its laws will come crashing down on you as go crashing down to the ground. The only one who can defy those laws is the one who created them: God.

There once was a man named Elisha who witnessed a man named Elijah defy the laws of gravity at God's command and take off toward heaven in a chariot. God is the maker of the laws of gravity and is the only one that can break those laws. Therefore, trusting in Him to do what we deem impossible makes sense because He's better than exact science.

This is what David did. He didn't care what everybody was saying about Goliath. Goliath was just a man God made. I'm sure David was thinking, "God created you, and you're going to speak against your maker? I'm not having it! This disrespect stops here and now!"

That's how we must feel when the enemy tries to throw all manner of negativisms and demotivating thoughts our way. Since we know that the enemy is a liar, we must confront him with God's word of truth about us and our situation. Sometimes, just for good measure, throw in how you've read that his future doesn't look too bright.

Call in Reinforcement:

The problem with our battle is that we speak more about our Goliath than we do of our God. We magnify our enemy and our problems instead of our God. I'm sure it may have been easier for David to come with a fresh perspective on the situation since he was not there being taunted day in and day out by the enemy. The enemy will try his best to wear us down with his lies and discouragement causing us to experience battle fatigue. That is the time when we call in reinforcements to assist us in our fight. We need to always have at least one person, if not more, who we can go to and ask them to hold up our hands when we're getting weary from the battle. These people may be our prayer partners, prayer warriors, friends in the Lord. David was the Israelite army's reinforcement.

Remembering Past Victories:

David had no idea he was going to a fight. He thought that he was delivering food for his brothers. Yet he was more ready than they were for the battle. His time alone with God and his previous experience with God had prepared him for the unexpected. Did you know your time with God can prepare you for the unexpected? So much so that when the unexpected comes, it can leave you upright. If you do occasionally get knocked off your feet, you will bounce back up so quickly, it may not even feel like you were down. Time spent with God builds up those "bounce back" muscles. We all need bounce back muscles because this life will bring to all of us things that will unsteady us and try to make us lose our footing.

Psalm 73:2 says:

> *But as for me, my feet were almost gone;*
> *my steps had well nigh slipped. KJV.*

If that's too King's English for you, the Good News Translation says:

> *But I had nearly lost my confidence;*
> *my faith was almost gone.*

Clearer? Yes, it seems that the Israelite army had lost their confidence in God. From the lowest soldier right on up to the King. No one was remembering and recounting what God had done for them in the past. We must never forget our past victories. We must never lose sight of what God has already done and the promises He has made to us. He is a Promise Keeper. Write down his word and your testimonies. Rehearse them over and over in your heart and in your mind.

> *Thy word have I hid in my heart that I might not*
> *sin against Thee. Psalm 119:11 KJV*

David said he would hide God's word in his heart. In times past, the Israelites were instructed to bind God's word on their hands and write them on the posts of their houses and gates. I don't know about you, but I'm glad that all I have to do is put His word in my heart for safekeeping. So happy that I don't have to write it on my house. Ain't nobody got time for that! David discovered this secret, applied it, and it worked.

The next time Goliath starts throwing empty threats at you, remind him Who your God is. When **"Er-Body's Talkin' Bout Goliath, and Nobody's Talkin' Bout God,"** change the conversation. You speak up and remind everyone within earshot Who your God is and the promises that He's made. You are qualified because you have put in the time. You have the Greater One on your side and in you. ***Never let the conversation of Goliath dominate your speech!***

Act-Ing Out Prayer

THE PERFECT ACRONYM TO PRAY BY

A = Adoration
C = Confession
T = Thanksgiving
S = Supplication

The word "ACTS" is such a perfect acronym to use as a prayer guide. The fact that it is one of the key books of the bible and also means, 'to take action; do something', just adds further to its use here. It's like the letters in the book of ACTS were made for this guide on how to approach God in prayer.

Adoration: It starts with giving honor to God, a*doring* Him. We must never forget to love on God. What father does not want to be loved on and adored by his children? We can never out-love Him, so don't worry about over doing it. Before going any further in our prayer, we should first acknowledge Who He is and our dependency on Him. Our Father Who art in heaven. Hallowed be Thy name. Thy kingdom come. Thy will be done. On earth as it is in heaven. Father, we adore You simply for Who You are.

> *"O Come let us worship and bow down: let us kneel before the Lord our maker" Psalm 95:6 KJV*

Confession: Confession, they say, is good for the soul. Confess, ask forgiveness, and move past it. If you dwell too long on sin it will take you to a dark place. God sent Jesus as the propitiation for our sins so that we would not have to bear them ourselves. Know that He has forgiven you if you ask and truly plan not to return to it. **Do not try to punish yourself.** Then for what purpose did Jesus die and take your punishment?

But I believe this confession is not just a confession of sins, which we should do. We must also confess our utter need for and dependence on Him. This kind of confession is also a consistent profession of faith and gratitude for His goodness lest we forget. Father, I *confess* that You are God and God alone and above You there is no other. I *confess* that I need You daily in my life. I *confess* that I cannot complete my earthly assignment without Your guidance. These are just a few. I'm sure you can think of many others because He is such a good, good Father.

> *"How great is Your goodness which You have stored up For those who fear You, which You bestow in the sight of men On those who take refuge in You" Psalm 31:19 NIV*

> *"Repent, then, and turn to God, so that your sins may be wiped out, that times of refreshing may come from the Lord"* Acts 3:19 NIV

Thankfulness: To this, there is no end. Thanking God is more personal because we each have our own list of individual blessings we can thank Him for along with the things we have in common, such as the air we breathe, food to eat, a roof over our heads, etc. I can think of far more things to thank Him for than I can think of to ask Him for. His goodness to His children is infinite and far-reaching from generation to generation. I personally thank Him for sending His Son Jesus to die a death that would bridge the gap between God and man forever. This is our voluntary and eternal task. You will find that the more grateful you are, the happier you'll be.

> *"Gratitude is the healthiest of all human emotions. The more you express gratitude for what you have, the more likely you will have even more to express gratitude for". —Zig Ziglar.*

> *"Give thanks to the Lord, for He is good; His mercy endures forever"* I Chronicles 16:34 KJV

Supplication: The S for Supplication falls in place last, as it should. Don't get me wrong. I have nothing against asking God for His blessings and His sustenance. He said, "You have not because you ask not and when you ask, you ask with wrong motives." He owns the cattle on a thousand hills and the hills that they graze on. So, He certainly has everything we need. But I think that this acronym puts asking in its proper place. Most dive right into asking before we acknowledge Who He is and thank Him for what He's already done. Never fail to ask and keep on asking. Seek and keep on seeking. Knock and keep on knocking. If you do this, what you ask for will be given to you, what you seek you will find, and the door that you're knocking on will be opened for you (Matthew 7:7 and Luke 11:7). Healing, salvation of lost loved ones, restoration of broken marriages, and success in job and business ventures are available to those who will be so bold as to ask. Anything we need, He promises to supply. Yes, He already knows exactly what you need, but He wants to engage with you. So do ask Him for what you need. But always make sure your asking lines up with His word.

> *"And all things you ask in prayer believing you will receive" Matthew 21:22 KJV*

After all of these are done, we need to quiet ourselves before Him to hear what He has to say to us. Because what He has to say is significant to the accomplishment of our journey and consequential to the success of completing our assignments. So many people have gone to their graves without completing their assignments because they left this key component out. <u>LISTENING</u>. If we do all the talking how will we ever receive instructions? Since our assignment comes from Him, it would make sense to get direction from Him on how it is to be carried out. The only way to do this is to listen intently and intentionally to the directions and instructions He will, without fail, give us.

In conclusion: Speak to God often. There is no special speech you must use. Just speak "You." However you speak is what He wants to hear, and He perfectly understands your language. He is anxiously waiting to hear from you and to talk to you.

So, **A**dore Him. **C**onfess your faults *to* Him and your love *for* Him. **T**hank Him always and for all things. **S**upplicate or ask and keep on asking until He says no, wait, or supplies your desire. Live righteously before Him. When you fail to do this, as we all do from time to time, get up and dust yourself off. Know that He will and has forgiven you, then get back to your assignment. Cry if you must, but never stop moving forward. And oh yeah, don't forget to listen for direction. Let His word, His love, and His leading guide your path.

Acknowledgements

Mom: Thank you Mom for always encouraging me to use the gifts that God gave me. You've always been there for me.

Esha: I appreciate you for letting me lean on you for so many of my technical needs. You never demean my technical illiteracy. Always willing to help whenever you can. Thank you.

Shay: I love the way you see the best in everyone. You have encouraged me to keep going, saying, just because it's been done before doesn't mean I can't still do it. Thank you.

Ri': your words were always encouraging. Negativity is not in your DNA. Thank you for believing in me and what I was trying to achieve.

Mike Jr: because of distance, you have not had to be privy to the ups and downs of this journey, but I can still hear your voice urging me on.

Joyce: Your editing assist was by far a blessing. But mostly your encouragement and belief in me was empowering. Thank you

Debi R: your excitement each time I would mention to you that I was writing a book was contagious. You will never know how much your enthusiasm about it has meant to me.

Chef Cheree: it was your obedience to God in sharing the word that He had given to you for me that started me on this journey. Thank you from the bottom of my heart.

Appendix

Section 2, The Call: God is Not Out To Get You was written for my brother David Nelson

1st line 9th stanza: The Victory is in Your Mouth was taken from her book, 'I'm Done With Either Or Thinking' by the co-Pastor of Faith Christian Center/FCC, Erica Renee Moore

2nd line 3rd stanza: 'Run Toward Your Fear' is a familiar Joyce Meyer quote.

The poem RHU was given to me for a young woman at my church who had just graduated ministry school.

I Still Have Room was my birthday gift from my Daddy on the morning of my birthday and was gifted to me and completed in approximately an hour after I began my morning worship.

Statistics in 'Don't Let This Melanin Fool You' were quoted from the June 1st 2010 online article of HealthLeadersMedia.com titled, RACE MATCHING IN TRANSPLANTS DOES NOT IMPROVE SURVIVAL.

The 'People of Victory' definition of NIKI was found at www.thinkbabynames.com > meaning.

Nicky as a girls name (also used as a boys name Nicky) is of Greek and English origin, and the meaning of Nicky is "People of Victory". Nicky is an alternate spelling of Nicole, (Greek) from Nicola. Nicky is also a derivative of Nikki (English). Associated with Greek victory.

Variations:
Nykia, Niko, Nikky, Nikkie, Nikkey, Nikia, *Niki*, Nico, Nickye, Nickie, Nicki.

About The Author

Amara Alexander is the mother of four adult children, nine grandchildren, and one great grandson. She married at the age of 18. Her marriage survived 4 decades but was dissolved in 2016. In the process of re-establishing her life again, God was able to regain her full and undivided attention. It was then that she began to see what He had been trying to show her all along; and that is that He was not done with her and that He still had use for the gifts He had placed in her. She states that she has been humbled and could not have imagined all that was locked inside her waiting to be released as evidenced by her piece, 'I'm So Pregnant'. It was due to God's repeated reminder that He'd said to her, **"This Time Keep Going"**, and because of the early morning meetings with Him, that this book of poems and short pieces have been written.

CPSIA information can be obtained
at www.ICGtesting.com
Printed in the USA
BVHW090928240221
600911BV00017BA/1397